deposition | dispossession

D1191259

deposition | dispossession

Climate Change in the Sundarbans

Marthe Reed

Introduction by Angela Hume

Kelsey Street Press

Kelsey Street Press

2824 Kelsey Street, Berkeley, CA 94705

www.kelseystreetpress.org

Library of Congress Cataloging-in-Publication Data

Names: Reed, Marthe, author. | Hume, Angela, writer of introduction.

Title: deposition | dispossession : climate change in the Sundarbans /
Marthe Reed ; introduction by Angela Hume.

Description: Berkeley, CA : Kelsey Street Press, [2021]
Includes bibliographical references.

Summary: "deposition | dispossession: Climate Change in the Sundarbans,"
the posthumously published work by Marthe Reed, responds to the ecological
crises of the Sundarbans of south Bangladesh and India.—Provided by publisher.

Identifiers: LCCN 2021010885 | ISBN 9780932716910 (paperback ; acid-free paper)

Subjects: LCSH: Sundarbans (Bangladesh and India)—Poetry.
Climatic changes—Poetry. | Human ecology—Poetry. | LCGFT: Poetry.

Classification: LCC PS3618.E43566 D47 2021 | DDC 811/.6—dc23

LC record available at https://lccn.loc.gov/2021010885

Designed by Crisis

Typeface designed by Namrata Goyal

Cover artwork by Marthe Reed

Edited by mg dufresne, Carla Hall, and Vanessa Kauffman Zimmerly
with editorial support from Laura Mullen and Jill Stengel

Special thanks to Mike Kalish

Printed on acid-free, recycled paper
in the United States of America

Contents

*"Can text *touch*"?*

An Ecopoetics of Reaching and Recognition for Turbid Waters

Marthe Reed's seventh full-length book of poetry, *deposition | dispossession: Climate Change in the Sundarbans*, takes readers to one of the most biodiverse and also most threatened ecosystems in the world: a tidal wetland forest delta in eastern India and Bangladesh.[1] As Reed's title suggests, *deposition | dispossession* explores the ways in which climate change and other human impacts have ushered in an era of unprecedented volatility and violently diminished the life chances of humans, animals, and plants in the Sundarbans.

Home to the largest remaining mangrove forest in the world, the Sundarbans islands span approximately 10,000 sq. km (4,000 sq. mi.).[2] They are located where the freshwater Ganges Delta empties into the saltwater Bay of Bengal. For centuries, tides have submerged much of the islands and then retreated on a daily basis.[3] Today, the Sundarbans is a climate change hotspot.[4] As the climate warms, tropical storms and flooding are intensifying in the region, and coastlines are col-

---

1. Susmita Dasgupta, Istiak Sobhan, and David Wheeler, "The Impact of Climate Change and Aquatic Salinization on Mangrove Species in the Bangladesh Sundarbans,"*Ambio* 46 (October 2017): 680.

2. Ibid.

3. Ari Shapiro, "The Vanishing Islands of India's Sundarbans," NPR, May 23, 2016, https://www.npr.org/sections/parallels/2016/05/23/478393443/the-vanishing-islands-of-indias-sundarbans.

4. Manon Verchot, Indrani Basu, and Joanna Plucinska, "Between the Dark Seas and Living Hell," *Huffington Post India*, July 1, 2016, https://projects.huffingtonpost.in/sundarbans/.

lapsing. In the coming years, millions of human inhabitants will have no choice but to migrate.[5]

A former resident of the US Gulf Coast—also vulnerable to destruction from extreme tropical storms and human development, as the poet well knew—Reed looked across the world to the South Asian mangrove forest and asked: how can one imagine, touch, care for, and write about an amorphous landscape and precarious ecology geographically distant from one's own? Of her feeling of geographic distance, Reed writes, "I do not have a reliable map, only proliferating lists, slips of papers. [H]alf the Sundarbans lie submerged during monsoon" (27).[6] In the absence of a map, Reed asks, can one "touch data" (40)? That is to say, "can text *touch*" (42)?

Motivated by these questions, Reed explores a poetics and ethics of *reaching toward*. This reaching toward manifests as a lyric study in fragments. Additionally, one might describe Reed's project as a work of documentary ecopoetics, thus situating her book in a tradition that extends from Muriel Rukeyser to Myung Mi Kim and M. NourbeSe Philip.[7] Reed's spare lyricism is also resonant with Lorine Niedecker's mid-twentieth century Objectivist poetry of the floodplain.[8] Reed arranges her language, culled from news stories and scientific reports, sparsely on the page. At times phrases, words, and letters drift from the page's margins, as though swept up by the rising tide, perhaps deposited as silt in the tide's retreat. She also makes use of unconventional punctuation. Reed repeatedly inserts a double colon (::),

---

5. Shaberi Das and Sugata Hazra, "Trapped or Resettled: Coastal Communities in the Sundarbans Delta, India," *Forced Migration Review* 64 (June 2020): 15–17.

6. All notes and poetry attributed to Marthe Reed throughout this introduction are from Marthe Reed, *deposition | dispossession: Climate Change in the Sundarbans* (Berkeley: Kelsey Street Press, 2021).

7. For an illuminating statement on documentary poetics, see Myung Mi Kim, "Pollen Fossil Record," in *Commons* (Oakland: University of California Press, 2002), 107–111.

8. For more on the "flexible, provisional practice of mid-twentieth-century open form poetry," see Samia Rahimtoola, "'Hung Up in the Flood': Resilience, Variability, and the Poetry of Lorine Niedecker," in *Ecopoetics: Essays in the Field*, ed. Angela Hume and Gillian Osborne (Iowa City: University of Iowa Press, 2018), 189–207.

among other marks and shapes. The effect is a heightened materiality of the page, a turbidity or silty-ness. Through her material poetics, Reed attempts to transgress physical distance and also the challenge of imagining, to such a degree that it begins to feel almost like touching, a faraway environment.

deposition | dispossession opens with an invocation of the poet's muse:

> *Sundari* tree
>
> "beautiful"
>
>
> "forest"
>
> (7)

Sundari, meaning "beautiful" in Bengali, is the dominant mangrove species in the Sundarbans. Its root systems help stabilize coastal areas and protect against erosion. Here the word itself takes root, grounding the poem and the reader. The next words on the page echo, ebb, and flow, registering the watery transience of the floodplain. Two pages later, Reed writes, "animals arrive with the tide . . . out of reach—roots, limbs, topmost leaves . . . v a n q u i s h e d   i n   t h e   f l o o d" (9). The words, too, become flooded and come apart, indicators of the "contour / of flood" (12).

The spareness of Reed's poetry and ample white space on many of her pages convey the "drench" state of the Sundarbans (12). Her compressed couplets often suggest images of ecological disturbance:

> river convergence
>
> pools
>
> eddies
>
> sharp meanders
>
> "blind"
>
> in turbid water
>
> (14)

These lines likely reference the Ganges and Brahmaputra rivers, which converge at the Ganges-Brahmaputra Delta and empty into the Bay of Bengal. This delta is one of the most fertile regions in the world and also one of the most populous.[9] Human activities such as damming, exploitation of mangrove timber, and industrial pollution continue to alter the topography and hydrology of the rivers and the basin.[10] Currently, the Ganges and Brahmaputra are meandering eastward, which is affecting sedimentation and reducing freshwater inflow.[11] Sometimes exacerbated by damming, meander bends in a river can contribute to greater erosion. Moreover, rising sea levels are contributing to aquatic salinization in a region that already faces seasonal freshwater shortages.[12] In this context, Reed's couplets read like turbid water themselves, thick with references to shifting ecological processes.

Throughout the book, Reed names threatened species of the Sundarbans, including the vulnerable Irrawaddy dolphin, "critically . . . imperiled" (17), and the Bengal tiger, who, while globally endangered, in the Sundarbans makes up the largest remaining wild tiger population in the world.[13] With climate change and consequent rising sea levels, these tigers have seen the decline of their habitat. They are also threatened by poaching and the harvesting of their prey species and other resources in their areas.[14] Scientists predict their habitats will be mostly wiped out by 2050, leading to their extinction by 2070.[15] Reed addresses the violence caused by the greater proximity of tigers and humans in the Sundarbans:

---

9. "Ganges–Brahmaputra Delta," Delta Alliance, accessed January 26, 2021, http://www.delta-alliance.org/deltas/ganges-brahmaputra-delta.

10. Dasgupta, Sobhan, and Wheeler, "The Impact of Climate Change," 681.

11. Ibid.

12. Ibid.

13. Sharif A. Mukul et al., "Combined Effects of Climate Change and Sea-level Rise Project Dramatic Habitat Loss of the Globally Endangered Bengal Tiger in the Bangladesh Sundarbans," *Science of the Total Environment* 663 (January 2019): 831.

14. Ibid., 837.

15. Ibid., 838.

(tiger

) widow

at the village

margins

(21)

As climate change alters the bioregion, human inhabitants are increasingly being driven into the tigers' habitats. And as humans try to adapt their lifeways, these collisions will continue to occur more frequently. One example has to do with honey collection in the jungle. Researchers think that, as mangrove species distributions shift as a result of climate change, some parts of the forest will likely see more honey production and, as a consequence, more human honey collection.[16] But more honey collection will likely mean more human-tiger conflicts in the forest.[17] More conflicts will lead to greater numbers of humans being killed by tigers, and then possibly more retaliatory killings of tigers by humans.[18] Reed's open parentheses suggest how tigers and humans are pulled and pushed toward each other by material forces beyond their control.

One might bring together the words "tiger" and "widow" to make the phrase "tiger widow." Reed's next lines begin to tell of the situation of women in the region who have lost their husbands to tiger killings. These "tiger widows" are believed to

---

16. Dasgupta, Sobhan, and Wheeler, "The Impact of Climate Change," 690–691.

17. Ibid., 691.

18. Mukul et al., "Combined Effects of Climate Change," 837.

bring

bad

luck

(46)

The tiger lives nearby, at the village "margins" or edges, and women who are believed to bring bad luck are ostracized, or marginalized, in their own villages. These lines also point toward the larger-scale precarity and marginalization of women in the Sundarbans, which Reed confronts head-on when she writes:

dis-

placed

women

sex

workers

feeding

their families

(71–72)

According to a 2016 article that Reed cites in her book, with more dramatic annual flooding and weather events, Sundarbans islanders are being forced to migrate to cities such as the West Bengal capital Kolkata to seek refuge and employment.[19]

---

19. Verchot, Basu, and Plucinska, "Between the Dark Seas and Living Hell."

Increasingly, they arrive to a saturated job market. As a consequence, women who have lost their husbands and have children to care for, many of whom call themselves "bhasha" ("flooded") people, are more often turning to sex work in the city's red-light district.[20]

In his book *The Great Derangement*, Amitav Ghosh points out that human residents of the Sundarbans "were ecological refugees long before the term was invented."[21] Throughout history, humans, among them Ghosh's own ancestors, have had to reckon with and adapt to the dramatic cyclical changes that occur in the delta region.[22] But as "the accelerating impacts of global warming have begun to threaten the very existence of low-lying areas like the Sundarbans," Ghosh observes, writers—fiction writers in particular—are coming up against formal and narrative challenges as they attempt to represent the changing climate on the page.[23]

Reed's *deposition | dispossession* grapples with the challenges that climate change poses to the human imagination not through fiction but through poetry, a genre that, Ghosh argues, "has long had an intimate relationship with climatic events."[24] One might say that fiction writers and poets alike now face unprecedented conceptual challenges as they attempt to write about the almost unthinkable implications of climate change indicators. But perhaps Ghosh is right in suggesting that poetry is well suited to the task, as it is unbeholden to narrative in ways that fiction can be and, moreover, has long been mobilized by poets themselves to convey extreme weather events.[25] Notably, poetry today is wildly various

---

20. Ibid.

21. Amitav Ghosh, *The Great Derangement: Climate Change and the Unthinkable* (Chicago: University of Chicago Press, 2016), 3.

22. Ibid., 6.

23. Ibid., 7.

24. Ibid., 26.

25. Ghosh cites Geoffrey Parker on John Milton, who, Parker points out, started writing *Paradise Lost* during an extremely cold winter and then made climate changes central to his poem. See Ghosh, *Great Derangement*, 26.

in its trajectories and impacts, not unlike climate change itself, perhaps further contributing to its potential to help humans imagine new environmental realities.

Crucially, Reed's poetry evades narrative. While many things *happen* in the book—for example, the flood "eats" and species "adapt"—it does not tell a linear story about climate change. Instead, *deposition | dispossession* attempts to formally attend to and register the nonlinear, cyclical ebb and flow that has long defined the Sundarbans' ecology: the deposition, or accumulation, of sediment left in the tide's path, and also the dispossession, or stripping away, of habitat in the flow and flood. As Myung Mi Kim writes in a poetic essay about her own documentary ecopoetics, "The book emerges through cycles of erosion and accretion."[26] Certainly, this description is applicable to Reed's documentary ecopoetics as well. *deposition | dispossession* evokes how the Sundarbans' ebb and flow has always been and simply *is*, while also naming climate change's devastating realities:

> *when*
>
> *marine mammals*

((*when*

begin to disappear

(77)

And then:

no

clean water

no

---

26. Kim, *Commons*, 107.

food security

no

cultivatable land

(80)

These lines bring the meaning of dispossession into sharp relief. Climate change threatens to eradicate island species and render the Sundarbans uninhabitable for humans. An implicit question of the book is: how does one write poetry for a disappearing place? Reed's answer, it seems to me, is that one must attempt to *touch* the threatened place using poetry that calls attention to the materiality of the poem's language and also the materiality of the place to which the poem refers. Thus, Reed reveals her faith in the twofold power of poetry: first, to demonstrate the potential impact of language in a time of planetary crisis and, second, to model reaching toward—that is to say, bearing witness to an endangered place in its persistent material being—while there is still time to act.

In this sense, *deposition | dispossession* exemplifies a poetics of what Lynn Keller names "the self-conscious Anthropocene." For Keller, the phrase "self-conscious Anthropocene" describes a historical period and cultural phenomenon of "changed recognition" in which humans possess a "reflexive, critical, and often anxious awareness of the scale and severity of human effects on the planet."[27] This sensibility is borne out by poetry. In contrast to earlier nature writing, Keller argues, the poetry of the self-conscious Anthropocene "resists being approached as an escape from the problems of a warming, toxified world."[28]

Reed's poetic awareness is certainly critical. Descriptions of destruction caused

---

27. Lynn Keller, *Recomposing Ecopoetics: North American Poetry of the Self-Conscious Anthropocene* (Charlottesville: University of Virginia Press, 2018), 2.

28. Ibid., 11.

by climate change share a page with a citation from the US government's refusal to fund climate change research. Another page points to the responsibility of the United States for disproportionately high emissions (81). Moreover, in its awareness, Reed's poetry is *insistent* that reaching and recognition—what Ghosh describes as "the passage from ignorance to knowledge" when "a prior awareness flashes before us, effecting an instant change in our understanding," or "renewed reckoning"[29]—are the beginnings of any environmental activism.

Before we humans can change our understanding, we first have to be able to touch the "beautiful forest." That is to say, we must feel in touch with the deep time, cycles, and ruptures of the planet. Only then will the diverse ecologies within our world ecology become real to us. As Reed shows, poetry can help bring our imperiled world into the realm of the real, and thus, through reaching and recognition, poetry can begin to change our minds.

Angela Hume
San Francisco, 2020

---

29. Ghosh, *Great Derangement*, 4–5.

deposition | dispossession

I think that measuring with precision human activity on the climate is something very challenging to do and there's tremendous disagreement about the degree of impact, so no, I would not agree that it's a primary contributor to the global warming that we see. But we don't know that yet, we need to continue the debate and continue the review and the analysis.

—United States Environmental Protection Agency Administrator
Scott Pruitt (served February 17, 2017–July 6, 2018)

Doubtless there are questions you would like asked. What are they?

—Wendy Burk

Make the *green world* stop.

—Bhanu Kapil

Sundari tree

"beautiful"

"forest"

sea

forest

animals arrive with the tide

a muddy color
flux of fresh and salt

out of reach—roots, limbs, topmost leaves

shundâr bôn

v a n q u i s h e d   i n   t h e   f l o o d

"waste country"

tide lands

fields of mud

::

depositional scrub

land

spotted
deer pick

their way
inland

through pricked
pneumatophores

drop and
prop roots

stilting
in anoxic silt

what is expected

a tide moving north then south
south

and north

contour
of flood

drench

and the memory of drench

200 m i l e   r e a c h

Bay of Bengal

green's e f f l o r e s c e n t

body

drowning

Gangetic   side-
swimming

"extreme
ecological specialization"—

      river dolphin
         upstream

with the tide
relict

lineages counter-
currents

river convergence
      pools

        eddies
   sharp meanders

"blind"
 in turbid water

river
habitat

light and dark

a habit of
lunar response

ancient ruin
Lady

Bon Bibi's[1] house
*in*most

island
gifts of redress

or blessing tiger
prophylaxis

1. "Lady of the forest," a protective spirit or guardian against tiger attack.

what do I say about beginnings?

Irrawaddy dolphin

unfused cervical
vertebrae || pointed teeth

gently rotate
one eye
                        up

                                                inverted
                                cone of diminishing light

alone or
clustered in twos
or threes

short-beaked and
critically

                                                imperiled
                                confluence pools

                                        circling
                        away from the current

"jowar"

lost   in the flood

orcaella   echo-
locating
fish   crustaceans   mollusks young
turtles

submerged roots
branches
trunks

Sundari trees

tide flowing
2 0 0 m i l e s

inland
swallows the forest
a habit of green

islands
made or

unmade in a day

muddy and milky white

Ganges

Brahmaputra
Raimangal

Shela Bhola Meghna Baleswari Harinbanga

"fiery mouthed"
Agunmukha

Padma and Matha

beginning in water

::

when the stories are forgotten

the river remains

harrow the islands

flood
and retreat

no (known)
predators

except

humans

(tiger

) widow

at the village

margins

hem of her sari

trust

reciprocity

kinship

::

ritual
and migration

an unpredictable loss will occur

sunlight
takes form in shadow

dam-building siltation   increases
salinity

enmeshed in fry nets
((shrimp) farming

Irrawaddy
population decreased by

30%

3 generations
Ganges

50%

::

drowned
and flooded

body

panicles of pink or orange bell-formed flowers
Kali's ãchol

Sundari

"sea   forest"

nothing happens

every thing

200 years

ebb and flood

6000 square miles
reduced
to
1600

marginal marshes

sandbars

islands

tidal channels

Bengal tigers swim
island-to-island hunting

chital deer barking deer wild pig
less than

< one
meter

above sea level

I do not have a reliable map, only proliferating lists, slips of papers. half the Sundarbans lie submerged during monsoon. a green revolution. four of six local salt-tolerant strains of rice no longer extant, rain-fed paddy agriculture

nothing escapes the tides

4 million depend
on the forest

Sundarbans *sea forest*
to live

::

of climate change

"a common sorrow"

::

a coast in retreat
660 feet per year

sea level rise
twice

the global average
a place of

transition

full moon
in fog

::

who decides?

how?

ground to fine silt the earth becomes something else. subsidence deposition sub-
sidence deposition, crabs in multitudes scrabbling over the mud. leopards, Java-
nese rhinos, wild buffalo all locally extinct

a map delineates an imagined moment, its information no more stable than the
basket-born earth of the village embankment. a house built again and again

"we are not spending money on that anymore"[2]

2. Mick Mulvaney, Director of the Office of Management and Budget (February 16, 2017–March 31, 2020)
for President Trump, March 2017, referencing climate change.

does the river dilate and contract with the tide? another spit, island, time. dozens of rain-made creeks proliferate through the delta, profuse and mutable realm. labyrinth, archipelago, forest

languages flood the Sundarbans

Bengali

English

Arabic

Hindu

Arakanese

what

 is

the

significance

of

there

remaining

a

single

wild

population

of

Bengal

tigers

bodies kept

safe

behind

enclosure walls

::

our only

ethical

necessity (?)

any (?) ethical imperative

living a scant

one

meter

above

sea

level

what do we think will happen?

islands form in concentric rings

mudflats mangroves gouged mudbanks

drowned

land

Sundarban sea levels likely to rise in excess of

one meter

by the turn of the century

foraging
in the wet

::

dolphins

gharials

mugger (or marsh
crocodiles

salt-
water crocodiles

tigers

sharks

::

men hunting

crabs in
Sundarban creeks

::

tarpaulin
shack

widows

the tide pushes *north*ward

denying me entry

I am not there

is this important?

what if I could touch

data?

the Bangladeshi Sundarbans will

likely reach a critical threshold at

SLR between 24 and 28 cm above

the year 2000 baseline

beyond 28 cm

Sundarbans tiger

population

declines

in a

non

line

ar

fa

s

h

i

o

n

geometric or exponential?
orders of magnitude

can text *touch*

perhaps I mean

reach

habitat

frag-

mented

in

patches

"all models estimate total

adult tiger populations

at less than . . ."

". . . less than

20"

the rate at which Sundari trees adapt
to increasing salt

and rising sea levels
remains

uncertain
forests display signs

of
col-
lapse

::

hunting

island-to-island

intent on its prey

village development encroaches
at the edge of the forest

::

"tiger
widows"

bring
bad

luck

"less than . . ."

"20"

approx.

50

years

thresh and
patch of marsh

mosquito netting
dresses the bed

if money

had

::

seining
finest mesh possible

tiger shrimp
spawn

::

shrimp farming

honey gathering
timber

harvesting
poaching

::

tea remains
out of reach

inhabitation
patterns of return

what is necessary?

"ecosystem
                    services"

::

protection from monsoons cyclones tsunamis

food

building supplies

fisheries

carbon

cycling

Sundarbans store
4.57 billion
tons CO_2

$79 billion
intl. market
2014

it

doesn't

exist

high tide

Raimangal i n f l o o d

::

imagine

the crush of mud

Every year

my house gets inundated

water from the river comes in

it breaks the house

I rebuild it
and it's again destroyed

I am drowning in the water but I cannot let go[3]

3. Rubil Saha, who lives in a mud hut with his two children on the island of Ghoramara, as quoted by Ari Shapiro, "The Vanishing Islands of India's Sundarbans," NPR, https://www.npr.org/sections/parallels/2016/05/23/478393443/the-vanishing-islands-of-indias-sundarbans.

secure from

sea level rise

a color impossible to describe

a shift in
weights
increases

cyclonic
activity

knowledge gleaned at a safe remove

home

shadow and light marble the Sundari leaves, scatter over clayey silt beneath the mangroves' aerial roots, leaves and boughs in half-eclipse. In *Travels in the Mughal Empire*, Bernier offers a first-European description of the Sundari 'sea forest.' Bernier will later go on to invent 'race'

document of an "unmarked" place

laden with crab traps

fishing nets

hunting

men paddle *naukas* into forest reserves

      island to island

men

intent on

taken by tiger

Gangā Sagara

s
    p
      i
        l
         l
           s

        into

                    Bay of Bengal
                    chanted

her name relieves poverty
banishes

                    bad dreams
                    mother of outcasts

inexhaustible ::
thirtha meaning

"crossing place"
b e t w e e n

sacred and mundane
a ford in the river

a climate
threshold

nobody dared look there

does fear keep one alive?

the river was angry

took away so many things

it took away people's lives

children were swallowed

my home was gone

we had to leave[4]

4. Ratan Maity, as quoted by Ari Shapiro, "The Vanishing Islands of India's Sundarbans," NPR.

reliant upon the steady
arrival of petroleum
and natural gas

he has
never
heard of
melting polar
ice caps
or climate change

he is
unaware
sea levels
are rising
around
the world[5]

5. Ari Shapiro, "The Vanishing Islands of India's Sundarbans," NPR.

deep into the Bay of Bengal, the underwater course of the river e x c e e d s
the length of its terrestrial channel

Gangā's   hair

                    t a n g l i n g

                                        over the earth

the river
splintered
the embankment
tore away

huts
fields
trees

villagers

::

bhangon

breaking

descent
of the goddess

gangā
       desáhará

flowing between
three

worlds
watersnakegod

tumbles toward
Earth her force

channeled through
Shiva's hair

Ganga's
violence does not

break
the earth

waters it
river Shiva's

"water form"
three

snake | water terror | gift
      Ganga

            this

            translated

            world

Sundari
trees

Ganges
delta

drowned
and t e n d r i l l e d p r o f u s i o n

another
twilight Ganga's

blessing
bad dreams

the least of it
Jowar

flood eats
everything

even the ebb
one hundred and two

islands consumed by
(politics

sea and
salt   (g r e e d))

      waxy
elliptical

leaves adrift
     over its water

bhasha

f l o o d e d
      p e o p l e

Mousuni Island
West
Bengal

480 people
/mi²

far

beyond

eco
system
carrying

capacity

Every year, chunks of the 3,500 kilometre mud embankments collapse, and every year they are repaired with fresh mud.[6]

6. Manon Verchot, Indrani Basu, and Joanna Plucinska, "Between the Dark Seas and Living Hell," Huff-Post, July 1, 2016, http://projects.huffingtonpost.in/articles/sundarbans.

8300 acres 1969
7000 acres 2009

erratic monsoons
worsening cyclonic intensity
rising sea levels

5200 acres 2017

::

what sound does the water make flooding in from the sea?

expressed
as a carbon

dioxide equivalent

::

dis-
placed
women

sex

workers

feeding
their families

a body

kept

safe

a communal

what we might know

space

stranded

in

silt

ex-
posed to river action
as well as
waves

subsistence itself
threatened

::

what lives upon the mud?

how?

when
marine mammals

((when

begin to disappear

::

"Matla"

meaning
mud

to be still
and wait

tufaon

typhoon

still

no

        clean water

no

        food security

no

        cultivatable land

no

        health care

no

        schools

::

        one half
        population
        Sundarbans

U.S.
#1
source
total
warming

U.S.
27%
excess
atmospheric
CO_2

U.S.
4.4%
global
population

U.S.
41%
total
global
personal
wealth

U.S.
21%
global
greenhouse
gas
reductions

Our position on the Paris Agreement has not changed @POTUS has been clear, US withdrawing unless we get pro-American terms.

—Sarah Huckabee Sanders, White House Press Secretary
(served July 26, 2017–July 1, 2019), September 16, 2017, Twitter

If I

1.4

million

people

Sundarbans

Impact
Zone

touch it
does that make it

mine

to own or
owe

to make

way

::

rice sown in flood

low-caste

"untouchable"
re-
      settlement

               West

               Bengal

               forest

               preserves

::

this

        in-between

place

::

an accelerated
dispersal

idols

on a riverbank

a girl

::

carried off

by tiger

Marthe Reed authored seven books of poetry: *deposition | dispossession: Climate Change in the Sundarbans* (Kelsey Street Press, 2021), *Ark Hive* (The Operating System, 2018), *Nights Reading* (Lavender Ink, 2014), *Pleth* (Unlikely Books, 2013) with j/j hastain, *(em)bodied bliss* (Moria Books, 2013), *Gaze* (Black Radish Books, 2010), and *Tender Box, A Wunderkammer* (Lavender Ink, 2007). She also co-edited, with Linda Russo, *Counter-Desecration: A Glossary for Writing in the Anthropocene*, an anthology of essays and poetry, from Wesleyan University Press (2018).

Reed received a BA from the University of California, San Diego; an MFA from Brown University; and a PhD from the University of Western Australia. She was an assistant professor and the director of the Creative Writing Program at the University of Louisiana, Lafayette before becoming a humanities faculty fellow at Syracuse University in New York. She was also the co-publisher and managing editor of Black Radish Books. She died on April 10, 2018.